THE NATURE OF HUMANS:

Personal Growth through Poetry

CHRISTOPHER JONES

FriesenPress

One Printers Way
Altona, MB R0B0G0
Canada

www.friesenpress.com

Copyright © 2021 by Christopher Jones
First Edition — 2021

Additional Contributors:
Linda Beaulieu- Editor
Lisa Scott- Photographer
Clint White – Review

ISBN
978-1-03-911671-9 (Hardcover)
978-1-03-911670-2 (Paperback)
978-1-03-911672-6 (eBook)

1. BODY, MIND & SPIRIT, INSPIRATION & PERSONAL GROWTH

Distributed to the trade by The Ingram Book Company

Table of Contents

For my mother, Dorothy.

I'm sorry you never got to see your grandchildren.
You'd have been amazed.
This book of my poetry is for you. I think you would
have loved it.

Acknowledgements

I would like to thank my son Thom, and my daughter Charlotte, for their unconditional support and encouragement, especially over the recent years as I became more intentional about writing poetry. The love I have for you is deep and endless. I'm so proud of you both.

I extend unlimited love and gratitude to my wife, Lisa. Your gentle love and understanding allowed me to reveal myself through my poems with courage and vulnerability. It also encouraged me to write about how much I love you.

Big thanks and appreciation for the talents of my editor Linda Beaulieu, who nurtured my writing with thoughtful care and clear eyes and helped me create my very first manuscript.

Lastly, I'd like to acknowledge the caring support given to me by all the wonderful people at FriesenPress, a Canadian publisher with a big heart and much expertise, who have been dedicated to my success since we first met.

Introduction

If you have picked up this, my first book of poetry, I am humbled by your curiosity, grateful for your interest, and thankful to you for taking the time to walk through my lines with a full heart and an open mind.

I write about nature: the trees, the wind, and the ocean. About ageing, depression, and about love. I describe my self-discovery and the demanding and freeing transition to a better version of myself, my journey from intolerance, criticism and judgement to compassion and kindness and an acceptance of my imperfections. I write about human nature and how we are living unconsciously, victim to the stories we tell ourselves, believing them to be the only truth, holding us back from being our best selves that the world so desperately needs.

Becoming a business leader and then a leadership coach invoked in me a deep interest in human and leadership development. I began to explore adult development—how humans continue to develop throughout their lives (if circumstances permit) in distinct stages. This is also known as Vertical Development, an expansion of mindset or consciousness. It is the way we evolve ourselves, starting with self-awareness and the acceptance of all of who we think we are. More importantly we become aware of our thinking so that we can shift to becoming a witness to our thoughts, rather than identifying ourselves as our thoughts. This is truly an "Aha!" moment, and a big step forward in our personal (and professional) development. Without this realization, we can remain a victim of our narratives and emotions, running on autopilot from deeply held limiting beliefs. With this realization, we can notice our thinking and make different choices about what we say or do.

Humans are naturally evolving to higher states of consciousness, and therein lies the hope for humanity. As we come to accept our limitations and see the possibility of adjusting our perception of ourselves, of others and of the world, we become open to changing ourselves.

I write these poems for your interest, for your reflection, and to give you the opportunity to look inward to find solutions to the problems you see in the world. The world you experience is yours. You have created it and formed your perspectives and opinions about it, about yourself, and about other people. You do not have to be a victim to it. You are its author. You have unknowingly designed it, and therefore you can design a different view full of love, understanding and kindness towards yourself and towards other people. This is how you reveal your innate human compassion and empathy at a higher level of consciousness, and where you will find a far greater ability to deal with the complex and uncertain world in which we live. My hope for us all is to become fully conscious in our current state and to understand the enormous opportunity we have for humankind to achieve its destiny, our life's purpose: to evolve.

Part 1:

LETTING MY SELF GO

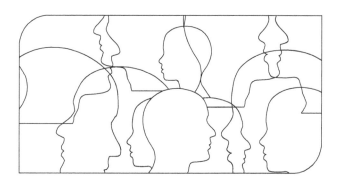

A Poem in my Pocket

I have the beginning
of a poem
tucked into
a small pocket
within a fold
of my mind.

An idea,
a phrase
or single word,
whispering.

A fragment
torn from the fabric
of my self;
a cringe, a rage,
an avoidance,
or an echoing despair.

The sadness
of a blinked tear
or a hope
gently budding,

Each one
escaping
into consciousness
with a small promise
and a potent urge
to belong.

Kite

I have a kite
and I really want to fly it.
It's carefully constructed
and very precious to me.
The attractive design
and bold colors
are appealing.
I think.

But what wind
will see it soar?
High and flowing
against the sapphire sky,
twisting and turning,
twirling in delight,
while I hold tight.

I'm afraid.
What if people
don't think much of it?
What if it's fragile
against the buffeting gusts
and opinions?
What if it dives and crashes,
or breaks free and flies away?

What if other kites
get noticed and admired
more than mine?

I think I'll just hold my kite
safe for now,
and watch all the others
dancing,
wondering what it's like,
wondering how it feels,
while I wait
for just the right wind.

Footprints

When I look back
I see the footprints
of my uncertain path,
some firmly pressed
by a confident stride,
others
hesitant in direction,
or lost.

When I look down
in reflection,
I see
a sharply pressed suit,
perfect for the opinion
of others.
For me,
the fabric of guilt?
The clothes of an imposter?

But now I begin
to comprehend
which is, in itself,
a shift of course.

Moved by a cold draught
of awareness,
I notice and grasp
the meaning of my footsteps,
the limitations
they represent.

As I peel off
each reluctant layer
of understanding,
the chill brings resolve
and purpose
to my tentative new steps.
Each new footprint
offering no leap forward,
but a soft surety
from each innocent toe.

The Leap

In an instant,
shorter than a breath,
here it is—
my stark opinion.
A lightning strike
from inner thunder
kicks aside curiosity,
stamps down compassion,
gets a foothold
and pushes off.
Sparked by righteous
knowing,
it leaps to judgment.

Landing heavily on both feet,
it stands, determined,
fists on hips,
a sneer of lips,
or the hint
of a fatalistic smile.
It has jumped;
fate sealed as a tomb,
quick as you dislike.

But now, at least,
I see it:
A shameful object
of my painful awareness.

So, I have begun
a different leap,
a softer touch,
a lighter tread
of hesitant steps
towards enlightenment
though it seems
a thousand miles distant.

Demotion

I am falling in love
with self-awareness,
where the gravity
of truth
pulls me down.

I seek a loving demotion
from my self,
from who I think I am,
a discrete deconstruction
of my inner form.

I want to find my true state,
the distillation
of my authentic essence.

I want to stop spinning
in my cocoon,
trapped
beneath dense layers
of deceit
and pretense.

I want to separate
from myself,
make my thoughts
an object

of my awareness,
my consciousness
comprehending
the unripe structure
of my mind

So I can accept
all that is,
so I can believe
in who I am,
so I can see
who I was always
meant to be.

Out of Tune

I hold an instrument
I'm trying to tune.
It's quite old,
a classic piece,
but cracked by dissonance.
It has no keys,
nor brass-funneled breath.

I think it has heart strings,
but plays mostly minor chords;
every note seems sharply
out of tune
or falls flat.

This instrument
is particularly delicate,
delightfully complex,
beyond even my attempts
to understand,
yet has the potential
to make the world gasp
at the beauty of its music.

I'm trying to tune in,
to fathom the depth of
the melody
and the harmony
I could invoke.

Beneath reason,
to the origin of the song —
the true composition
of the wonderful
instrument
I am.

Both &

An intake of air pauses,
then sighs an exhale
to complete a breath,
to make it whole.

It takes our earth
one full turn,
both night and day,
to finish a rotation.

I feel I am a contradiction,
sitting twisted
as an ampersand
in between the truth
of each opposite.

I can see,
yet I am blind.
I am awful,
and I am amazing.
I can love,
and I can hurt.

These polarities stretch me,
a tight sinew of thought
while the world demands

a binary answer—
yes or no,
no room for grey,
only black or white,
unable to hold both,
incapable of grasping
the paradox,
and considering each
as equals.

Yet each certainty
intersects in fragile balance
if you allow the duality
to weave together,
binding tentatively
in a single grasp.

Meanwhile I sit
with this understanding,
tangled and trying
to embrace my hatred
as much as my compassion,
to become my shadow
as well as my light.

Trying to feel
the love
at the center of it all.

Endless Chatter

I have discovered
I am not my thoughts
because
I hear them,
I see them
for what they are.
Tall tales
with a very
tentative commitment
to reality.

So, I seek myself
elsewhere.

I have found
that the buffeting
of my insidious
operating system
keeps me running,
blindly shoved
and lured
by the seduction
of productivity,
but no time for identity.

This industrious addiction
feels like chattering
across cobblestones
of empty purpose,
while I struggle to focus
my trembling eyes
on the distance
and my insight
on who I could be.

Looking for Myself

I've been looking
for myself—
the real one.

Wandering,
trying to find
the spark
I used to have.

Wondering,
what happened to
that fun-filled little boy
his bright face shining
with possibility?

I've become well shrouded
through the years,
but I'm feeling exposed
in my unravelling,
fragmented
by the deconstruction
of my significance,
reduced by the decline
in my value.

I've been looking
with head, heart, and will
to reveal
what's hidden,
to discover the truth
of who I really am.

With a mind as master
within my distended skull,
I'm desperately craving
a spiritual awakening
from somewhere within,
attempting to break free
from my safe, comfortable
trap
with all its false security.

But when I search
my dark corners,
I can't seem to illuminate
anything but shadows,
as black as the bruising
realization:
I know I can find myself
in your heart,

but not, it seems,
in mine.

Language

I live within
the language of my brain,
an existence
of harsh narratives
and determined conclusions.

Stories of fear and uncertainty
snag in my throat, full of doubt,
feeding my confusion,
questioning my opaque self-esteem.

So many conditions and rules
push me,
while I stumble to stay upright,
to function.

Exhausted from dragging chains
of productivity,
my addiction to insufficiency
sets me to task after task
while anchored
by a growing sense of futility.

My work,
endlessly draining,
is not my Work.
My compulsion to exceed

unwittingly builds more armor
to keep me in safe torment
protected by the certainty
of my obsession,
yet trapped by its insidious grip.

Critical

My lungs
fill with anxiety,
the caustic air
souring my tongue
and drying my teeth.
I stand, beaten,
braced against the chill
of a northerly
while storms boil inside.
A crash of thunder
with every annoyance
and no respite
from intolerance.
When I try
to crack a smile
at my disappointments,
my derision
merely grimaces.
My heart can't show me
a world
without the labels
of my cynical mind.
Disparaging opinions
are the authority,
ordering my verdicts
with a smirk of acid aversion,

while my compassion cowers
from the imposing dismissal.
I pause,
sink in
to the possibility
of a hopeful alternative
but my belly laughs
at my feeble attempt,
my distress liquifying
as the slate clouds
pour their scorn.

Deeper

I learned a trick
to empty my noisy mind,
which squawks constantly
with unhelpful thoughts.

If I place my palms
facing down
next to my head,
then lower them slowly,
the chatter falls away
(sometimes)
like particles of sand
through an hourglass,
pushing down criticism,
suppressing the
needless narratives.

As my hands
reach my jaw,
I start to picture
a level sea,
cerulean blue,
a cloudless sky above.

Now I can
feel into my heart,
slip into the ocean
and sense the wisdom
as I search the depth.

Quietness
and fading light
as I sink.
I seek a union
with my compassion,
my kindness,
my tolerance,
but my core
eludes the search.

Here?
No.
Deeper . . .
Here?
No.

My mind winces,
doesn't understand
(It was never meant to).

My heart speaks softly:
I am not in the ocean,
I am the ocean.

My Own Prison

I'm doing time
behind rigid lines
of black steel.
Trapped,
pacing,
wronged,
and faultless,
seething blame
through every gap.

But no-one listens,
no help comes.
No rescue
from my self-confinement.
Nothing to salvage me
from myself,
save pity.

Out there,
people are too busy
pointing accusations
from behind their own bars.

I'm drained
from my blind reaction
to the world
I think I see.
As my weary years
fall away
one by one,
revelation
shines a light
that radiates compassion,
understands me,
shifting my view
from accusation
to self-authorship
and a calm realization
of my opening.

Climb

I need
to climb.
To ascend
despite the lack
of reliable holds.
I have lots of rope
and all the gear
I could buy,
but I haven't
developed the skill.

I've read how
to rise,
how to use my knowing
and my shiny equipment
to scale the heights,
but I've never actually
made much effort,
apart from looking up,
never trusted myself
to take the first step.

I'm told
it's worth the exertion—
Worthy Work,
no matter how scary
or difficult.
Not for achievement,
nor to summit a peak,
nor check a box,
not for the workout,
nor the photo,

but to attain
a greater perspective,
a glorious elevation of spirit.
To achieve
an expanded view,
a heightened awareness
of all the world offers
just as it is,
beautiful and whole,
echoing resonant
with the wondrous silence
of love.

Harvesting Gifts in the Shadow

I have learned
if I want
to make others happy,
show them kindness.
If I want
to find joy,
show myself kindness.
But my protective mind
throws vindictive rocks
at my flinching heart
whenever I try.

How do I
reverse the tide
as waves of judgment
and stinging criticism
crash through me?

Apparently
I cast a shadow
of my self
below the foundations
of my mind.
I am beginning
to see it,
to feel it,
though it is deceptively dark.

How am I
supposed to
elicit wisdom
from this sinister stranger?
Claim my true gifts
when hidden
wounds from venomous barbs
drip through each day?

How am I to embrace
this gloom
with curiosity
and compassion?
Am I to be grateful
for these deeper gifts
I can barely reach
in the undercurrent?
I fear
I may drown
in the attempt.

Looking for Love

It's awkward.
I'm feeling clueless,
embarrassed
as an adolescent
looking for love.
Using my brain
seems to be
the wrong approach.
My flustered thoughts
cloud weak attempts
which get rebuffed.

Craving some
acquiescence
from my eager ego,
I gulp a breath
of courage
and try again,
only to flounder.

Ignored,
I wither
and reduce
to invisible shame.

Why is it so hard?
Especially when
I know exactly
who needs my love.

Not just anyone;
no stranger
with ice to break,
with a heart to melt.
How do I unlock
the heart I seek
when closeness
doesn't seem to count?
How do I learn
to love myself?

Swallowed

I've swallowed my self
and I'm choking on it;
pieces stuck
in my craw,
the rest
struggling down
into acid awareness
and the indigestion
it brings.
It's hard
to fully digest
who I am
without sourness
in my throat
and my eyes
watering.

My brain tells me
who I think
I should be.
I've done all
the reading;
it's not helping.

I want to listen
to the rest of me,
to tune in
and focus,
to see the screen
instead of the movie,
just in time
before my cinema reel
runs out,
flapping around
in the dark
hoping for help.

Autopilot

My hidden mind
relentlessly runs me
on autopilot.
This subconscious chauffeur
is reliable as breathing,
while a thousand
involuntary assumptions
muscle my regrettably
blind behavior
into limitless criticism
and judgement.

Untold
obstinate opinions,
watered and grown
from deeply buried beliefs,
need to be cut
and tied off
to stem the flow of
displeasure.

But despite
this thoughtless thinking,
these addictive attitudes
also hold rare gems
refracting
rays of hope,

each conviction
offering one gleaming letter
to form a shimmering word,
shaping bold expressions
that craft a new language,
the language
of my heart
that speaks
into a faultless world.

Heart Condition

I am my productivity,
and I've worked so hard
to unwittingly become it.
I am my knowing.
I am what others
want to see,
what my blinkered bias
tells me to be.

I've realized I have
a heart condition
and it's becoming critical.
If I don't learn how
to let it speak,
my dangerous disorder
will prevail.
My belligerent brain
will weld secure the identity
my shackled mind
has constructed for me
from the naiveté
of my selfish adolescence
and the innocence
of a wide-eyed
little boy.

To save myself
from this illusion,
I need to begin the Work
of unlearning,
of deconstruction,
of demolition
without the clarity
of a hammer.
I must erase
my blueprint,
learn to sever
each tightly tangled thread
in the neural web of lies
that creates my world.

The good news is
my heart is ready.
It always has been,
pumping patiently,
waiting for me to wake
and listen
to the meaning
of my life.

Geography

I need to uncouple
from the intricate
ecosystem
of my convoluted mind,
disentangle
from its deceitful hold,
its false security
and selfish intent.

I need to uncover
the geography of my heart,
explore the unknown landscape
as a wide-eyed stranger
looking for the place where
I belong.

I need to discover
the topography
of my declining form
down to my marrow.
Feel the awareness
in my untapped anatomy,
the vitality of my veins,
embrace the wisdom
in my bones
and discard the brittle fear
of dislocation.

I want to find
my spirit,
to know if I have
a soul-strength,
sense the core of my being,
recognize the very essence
of me
and know I am found
at last.

Our Quiet Compartments

We create containers
into which we quickly shrug,
or carefully put away
the unresolved pieces of our life.

A hundred voiceless compartments
hold the sealed baggage
we can't bear to face,
the pieces we don't
know how to assimilate
into the protected patterns
of our lives.

Each one securely stored
in tightly closed boxes
in the abandoned warehouses
of our minds,
or the forgotten crevices
of our hearts.

We package our grief
and our embarrassments,
our failures and our trauma,
keeping them locked away,
afraid of how they may
open us, how they might
shine a fracturing light

on the reliable world
we have constructed
for ourselves.

Our refusal to receive
protects us from wounds
their sharp edges would inflict.
But this denial breeds
a biting sadness
that we cannot resolve by
turning away.

Sacred and silent,
these banished fragments
sit hidden within us,
closed shrines to our
unbearable feelings,
pieces that want to alter us,
to evolve us, if we'd allow.

They quietly lie
drawn and curtained
by our ego's dismissals,
buried within us as a muted reminder,
pulsing in the folds of our being,
waiting for absolution
in the shadow of our avoidance.

These abandoned beliefs,
these unspeakable experiences
wait to be accepted,
to be heard, not avoided,
hoping for rescue,
for healing, or
for completion.
Craving breath to draw,
they wait to be seen, to be known,
to be accepted
and integrated within us.

Let us sense what is missing,
that which sits unresolved
or innocently saved
for another day.
Let us realize that
these are not caskets,
they are chests of treasure
full of unopened gifts
and ignored, hidden gems,
waiting to be held.

Until we face our closed doors,
unless we open up,
reach in and touch
the dark with an open mind
of consent,
and a heart of compassion,
we sit with the realization
that we

are our only hope for redemption,
for repair and resolution,
for closure that creates
an opening
to let all the light in.

Mind the Gap

I want to be
in the gap
between my thoughts,
to fall into
the opening
between
my stories.
I seek the pivot
between memory
and hope,
to stay in the brief lull
between
a moment ago
and
the next moment,
and exist
in the fleeting hesitation
between my past
and my future.

I crave
the sliver
of time,
the pause
between the seconds,
the chemical calm
before the spark

of neurons.
To settle in the beauty
of the silence,
when,
for an instant,
everything
stills,
falls away.

A state
empty of worry
and shoulds,
unoccupied
by my imagining,
devoid of all
except the purity
of presence,
of now,
this moment,
so I can experience
all there is
in the thin spaciousness,
the vast openness
of being,
and the sharp, delicate awareness
that all I am
is a single heartbeat
and an intake of breath.

Overwhelm (Bee Soup)

Often, my brain
seems to be
a nest of bees,
harried
and fully occupied.

It's hard to keep track
of a single notion,
apart from a sense
that one is angry,
another diligently caring
or full of
precious purpose;
hundreds of bumbling thoughts
a busy mess.

Other times,
my head seems full
of soup,
slopping
from ear to ear,
barely recognizable bits
floating.

I try to empty
my head.
An attempt at meditation,
leaving nothing
but silence,
pure presence
of being
in the moment,
but mostly
I'm stuck with
bee soup.

A Poem Takes Flight

Sometimes
a few words flutter
inside me
like startled starlings.
I feel the small push of air
in my chest
as tiny wings flap.

Distracted
and elusive
they scatter,
but then return
joined by others,
begin to coalesce,
to shape themselves,
then, unpredictably,
they change direction,
transforming into
a cohesive flock,

graceful and dramatic,
spiralling and flowing
as one,
they descend
and return to me
to gently hold
in my mind.

Both captured
and liberated,
soaring high,
dancing on the wind
until they become
distant specs . . .

B-Side

I've been playing
the music
of my life
unknowingly
from the B-side,
just glad to have
a single in the charts.
Problem is,
it's not so popular
with others.

The other problem is
I'm not sure how to play
the A-side.
In fact, I'm not sure
I've even heard it.

Sometimes a few faint notes
offer occasional
resonance,
some tentative tones
might catch people's ear.

It makes me wonder
how I could possibly be
full of song.

Part 2:

HUMANITY

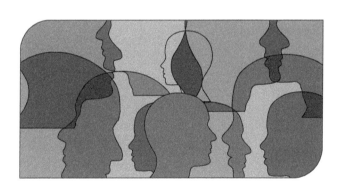

Look

We close our eyes
to dream,
to kiss,
and to feel.
We close our eyes
to despair,
or to reject
the opinions of others.
We close our eyes
to our pain,
to the pain of others,
and to die.
We close our eyes
to ourselves,
to our fears,
our flaws,
our longing,
and our failures.

We open our eyes
for attention,
for recognition,
to pretend,
or to look away.
We open our eyes
to our aspirations,
only to close them

on our intentions.
We could close our eyes
and open our hearts
to see ourselves.
To pause,
be present,
to reflect,
to look inside,
and notice
who we are
perhaps
for the first time,
and this time
not look
the other way.

The Child Inside

We dispute
our insignificance,
our inadequacy
and brokenness.
Cloaking it all
in arrogance
and expertise,
silence
or aggression.

We push fears away,
but are unable to
dismiss them,
so we turn
from our shadow
into the shine
of acquisition,
of fortune
and fake bravery,
wearing the characters
who show up
as circumstances demand.

Servants
to our false identities,
we erase the anguish
with social confidence
and laughter,
while the child inside
cries for attention
and the truth of us
gasps for air.

Black and White

Our firm perspective, a distinct opinion,
is less than half the story.
There's always more than my black;
your white, for example,
and all the grey in between.
There is always forgiveness to meet blame,
the virtuous to embrace the shameless,
simplicity to distill from complexity.

We don't feel the virtue of the friction
when opposites are poles apart,
yet we are the light that creates our dark
and allows us to see the alternative,
to embrace the pair, see unity in the polarity,
to seek the symbiosis and feel the need,
one for the other.

We feel we must select
one thing over the other.
Stand on one side
of a firmly drawn invisible line,
yet we were never meant to choose.
We can learn to accept both,
admit the wrong with the right,
see the hope that quells the fear,
find the gifts in each,
the balance of both.

Let us embrace what belongs together,
head and heart, your view
and mine,
just as the keys of a piano
under a gentle hand, both black and white,
form chords of major and minor
and combine in blended harmony.

Plenty

There's plenty of love in the world to go around,
we just need to organize it into all the right places.
Most of us have good intentions,
we just have to transform them into actions.

People do remarkable things every day,
from the goodness in their hearts,
to make others happy or grateful,
to create a new bond between people
that multiplies our human spirit.

There's way more good news in the world each day
than our screens would have us believe;
more belief, more joy, more happiness,
more tenderness, more tolerance,
more capacity to evolve, more open minds,
more giving, sharing, caring, supporting.

Have faith in humankind.
We all have a light that shines from deep within,
a luminescence of the heart ready to be opened,
and an unwavering purpose of resilience.

We each have special gifts and unique strengths,
an ability to love and be loved,
to bestow our life legacy to the world,
one we can freely give with no conditions,
only a deep desire to belong.

Love creates love.
Kindness and compassion from each of us
can heal the world
one embrace at a time,
with just a little intention
and a shoulder on which to rest our heads.

The Plunge

You cringe unintentionally
as icy fingers of fear grab you.
Hesitation grows like branches of anxiety
in your chest.

You dry swallow the acid
from your tongue, but then,
with a reckless spark of courage,
you p
     l
       u
         n
           g
          \\ e //
into the shock of cold water,
your closed face open to the pain,
the exhilaration of the liquid curve,
scything through fear
until the rising lifts you and
you fracture the surface.

Gasping with surprise,
you break the boundary
into clean air, back into life,
vibrating your emergence into
your own ripples.
Then, a second breath of realization,

a deeper experience fully felt
in every cell of your chilled body;

not for the dive,
but for the transformation
through cold fear,
for not succumbing,
for breaking through,
for changing the frequency
of this fear,
altering the relationship
you have with it,
for now, at least.

Discord

We stride with great intention,
to perfect
each uncertain note
in our composition,
hoping the facets of our life,
the sharps and the flats,
strike a vibrant chord
for others.
But when we attempt
to listen closely,
we cringe at
the lack of harmony.

We try to tune in,
fine-tuning our behavior,
but it still falls short
of a masterful rendition.
As we pause our steps,
cupping an untrained ear
to the sound,
it ricochets sharply
between wavering notes.

And yet, it is in this discord
at our imperfect edges,
in the uncertainty,
the break in the pattern

that snags attention,
that our interest is sharpened.

But we remain unsettled
by our performance
as the music
echoes awkwardly,
yet full of rich authenticity,
while we strain to hear
the bright song we are.

In Between

There's a gap
between theory and reality;
a valley
between thinking and doing;
a chasm after intention
and before action.

There's a difference
between talking about it
and acting on it.
There's a hesitation
of purpose
before it exhales
into accomplishment.

Why are we so stirred
by our aspirations,
only to file them away
in the corners of our mind?
Why don't our stories
crack open
to let out the truth?
Why do they dim
and turn opaque
before becoming real
enough to breathe?

What do we need
to connect the separation?
To close the opening?
What are we missing?
Is it courage,
or just initiative?
The lack of a catalyst,
or an absence of belief?
Or perhaps just the realization
that hope
needs a little help
to succeed?

A Different View

Hesitant as uncertain footsteps,
my words tread the line,
one cautious step
then another,
carefully crafting
a fresh outlook, then
transforming into
a daring dance,
a tango
of language.

My heart and mind unite
creating a new pathway,
an artery coursing
with vibrant vocabulary,
giving life
to imagination,
providing speech
to thoughts,
altering direction,
and offering a different view
on what you thought you knew.

The More we Give

I recoiled at the thought
of giving,
of sharing more,
judging others
who I thought
were not deserving
of my love.
I reserved it
for a sacred few;
those I was supposed to love
and those I truly did.

But this mindset of scarcity
limited my gifts,
and I failed to appreciate
how it confined me.
I set perimeters
wired with alarms
to signal any threat
to my vulnerability,
any attempt to steal
my tenderness.
I protected my love
because I believed

I had a finite amount,
rarely receiving enough
from myself,
assuming the supply
was scarce.

But now I see
the sad irony to this.
Now I finally understand
it takes loving
to appreciate our plentiful supply,
the fountain we are,
that the more we offer love,
the more we have
to give.

It's an illusion
that we must ration
how much we devote,
that we must carefully select
who we give access to,
because we're afraid
it might run out.
The truth is the opposite.
When we generously tender love
more is created,
the more abundant we are,
the more we can express
as an eternal source for others
and for ourselves.
A source

to fill the emptiness
and longing,
freeing us from seeking
a sad dependence on others
to provide the love we need,
realizing at last
we generate love
because we are
made of love.

Heartbeats

It seems
our primitive desire
is for life to be easy,
to accumulate things,
gather the people
we think we deserve
to make us happy
within our greed
and jealousy, but
without a requirement
for responsibility.

What sweet immorality
is this?
Discounting everyone
and everything
while we feed
our frenzied
but feeble attempts
not to lose.

Then I turn
to look at
myself.
I'm floored
to find myself
so flawed.

Where do I find
a balcony
from which to view
my life?

How many heartbeats
should I feel?
How many breaths
inside the rising
and falling
of my life,
within the womb
of our world,
before I cry out
and confront
my thoughtless
indulgence?

Notice

All things
offer themselves
to be lovingly captured
by our scant attention:
the warble
of a red-winged blackbird,
an aspen leaf shivering
its pale back
to the breeze,
a murmuration of starlings
coalescing in the evening air.
A glance of curiosity
or a tentative smile
in passing,
each one a gift
with no conditions.

Do we even notice?
Do we perceive
where we choose
to place the beehive
of our awareness?

Do we stop to gaze at
the billowing shoulders
of cumulus, shrugging
before thunder?
Do we smell the storm?
Feel an autumn tinge
in our nostrils?

Or do each of these moments
fall away without meaning,
while we search our screens
for something more important?

Something Missing

Do you get a sense
that something
is missing?
Have a feeling
there must be more?
Do you even know
what to seek,
where to look,
what's lost?

Something's unsettled;
an absence,
a feeling not quite right
in the pit
of your stomach,
in the depth
of you.
Despite everything,
there's a hollowness
packed full of unease
and concealed by being busy.

If only
you could redirect
your uncertainty,
your wondering,
towards reflection,

seeking inwards for identity,
for all you could be.
If only you could allow
a gentle release of
who you thought you were,
concede
a soft acceptance
of this unfamiliar state,
waiting with patience
for you
to see the world
differently,
and yourself
for the first time.

Tripwire

There are times
when we are triggered,
stumbling across
our own tripwire
thinking we were pushed.

Our reactions
tilt the world,
bending our mind
that falls victim
to their command,
drowning all calm
and spilling blinkered opinions
into our tunnel vision.

This lack of latitude
constricts all options
to a painful point,
a laser beam of red scorn,
pressured into service
by the sensitive snare.

We crash in,
commit to the crime
and fall to the flaw,
victim of our own ignition,
oblivious

to the burning sensation
that those near us feel,
then retreat from,
mostly with despair,
but sometimes with love,
as the tripwire
stretches taut
once more
in faithful devotion
to our failures.

The Pieces of our Life

We were made and we create ourselves
from all the pieces of our life,
the shapes and forms of our existence,
and the stories we produce,
patching them together as best we can,
with what we think we know,
not realizing the peril
in the dark cathedral of our mind,
nor seeing the doorway
at the back of our heart.

Our love, our light,
our life
is for us to choose,
if we choose not to be a victim
of ourselves anymore.
If we choose to see the beauty
of the whole, and, if we allow,
the unbounded possibility
we represent.

Down

I feel pressed by a persistent winter wind, my reluctance
    obliged to yield.
It plucks all the bright green leaves from my supple branch,
    one by one,
leaving only a skeletal twig. I feel dragged by a current that
    stops me
from standing, tugging at my confidence, altering my
    gravity. Blood
thins, shrinks from my fingertips to a soaking heaviness in
my heart, sinks to my stomach, and below. The
periphery glazes, reducing to a crystallizing core
of trapped distraction, tightly wrapped in
a fatalistic shroud. It sits me down with
leaden certainty as my day tilts, slips
sideways, and slides away, leaving
me raw in a cold fog, hoping for
a lamp. Am I to welcome this
dejection? To embrace it?
How can I, when I have
no warmth to
even
move?

Still Falling

She came to me
with the curiosity
of a fresh morning,
a shimmering sunrise
filled with milk-fed softness
and unconditional love.

Shining from within,
her face as bright
as a new day,
she offered
selfless giving,
all of who she is.
No tentative cloud
unsure about rain,
she poured
into my heart
with the flow
of a Rocky Mountain stream.

Born from the love
of mother earth,
she enveloped me
in the fullness
of her nature,

and so, I fell forward
into love
with the farmer's daughter.

Struggling
with myself,
with my confused shifts
and repetitive exertion
through a sun-cycled life,
I paused
as her self-authored love
opened me,
and into my unfolding
she rendered
her vibrant colors.

My pretty little prairie girl,
with the depth
of an Alberta sky,
held me
in a magnetic gaze,
with golden green eyes
like glistening sunlight
gilding new grass.
A look
that held me
as I sank
into its deep tenderness;
I feel I'm
still falling.

Grounded as rich earth,
her heart
as large as a red barn,
and as open.
She gleams
a transforming smile,
ever radiant
with all the sunrises
of her life.

With creative love
she nurtures
every leaf, stalk and fruit,
fur and feather alike.
Every human soul
is her community,
is in her garden
for her to sow seeds
of compassion,
her willing tears
moistening the soil
until everything becomes
soaked in her devotion.

Captivated
with the resonance
of her heart song,
I feel another gentle
drop of healing,
of renewal, with
every mesmerizing note,

filling me,
fulfilling me,
recreating me,
as I become
fully immersed
in the wonder
of her love.

Scorpion

There's something nasty
beneath my prickling scalp;
menacing, toxic,
waiting on a hair trigger
or the slightest breath
of distaste.

It's hidden in my brain.
A scorpion,
alive,
skulking within the crevices,
cramped
between my cranial folds,
trapped
with sinister intent.

Except the tail which,
with malevolent poise,
waits to strike
its sting of criticism.
I feel it
tense
whenever it's provoked.

This arachnid menace
hurts my head
while my heart cringes
in silence,
even though,
or perhaps because,
the poison
is aimed elsewhere.

Prisoner

As I silently engineer
my own delusions,
blind to the rift
with reality,
my sulking acceptance
lies beneath
the productive beast
of my toiling conviction,
keeping me a prisoner
of my disparaging
and exhaustive narratives.

These fear-fueled stories
keep me right here,
behind the ribs
of my confinement,
clenching my windpipe
as I hurt those I love,
trying to learn
to change,
to glimpse
the other side.

Attempting to emerge
but knowing I'm not enough
to believe in my release,
my warden mind not allowing
the insight of my heart
to show me the way out.

Ninety-Five

My dear old Dad,
crumpled and well worn,
wobbles
to his ninety-fifth birthday.
That's more candle than cake.
He now spends
most days
sitting in the lobby
of his care home
(ironically called Sunrise).
His uncertain eyes
blinking glaucoma,
glancing,
waiting
with muddled intent
and no clear purpose
while his remembering
dribbles away.
His cobwebbed brain
constantly misfiring
as the contents dissolve
through the decaying tendrils
of his mind.
Who he is
stumbles down the corridor
in confusion
and little dignity.

His horizon so foggy
he can't even see
his own sunset.

He wears five layers:
A vest,
two buttoned shirts,
a jumper,
and a coat and cap,
forgetting after
each goes on.
Every wrinkled piece
wondering about the
one underneath,
weaving a
cloth cocoon
as if
waiting for
his last transition.

He taught me,
if you're going to do a job,
do it well,
(taking the broom from
my inadequate hands).
He's certainly done
a good job
of getting old.

Now, as he drifts away
from us,
from himself,
I think of things
I haven't said,
he hasn't said,
because we didn't
know how,
and all the questions
I could have asked
when he was able
to answer.

Mortality

I circle
the mercurial seasons
for the sixtieth time
as my father sits dying,
slumped and wilting
with a befuddled stare.
His wits are ending
as he shuffles
across the surface
of a broader world
he no longer understands,
searching a mind
that no longer
comprehends.

It makes me think
of what I should be
thinking about
within my busy bubble.
What regrets does he have?
Is he proud?
Why didn't he tell me
that he loved me
when I know
he did,
in his way?

I love him still
for reasons
I cannot explain,
in ways
I cannot describe.
Maybe the way
I hold my jacket sleeve
with my fingers
just like he does,
or the way I see humor
in so much of life.

My world
is so much more
expansive
than his dwindling sphere,
yet he fails in mine,
so confused why
things
are not the same.
Not understanding
the pace,
the complexity,
from his pragmatic
and narrow mind.
Not even knowing
why anything
needed to change.

Perhaps
we all outlive ourselves.
Perhaps
we should be
able to conclude
when we're done,
rather than being
left on the platform
as the speeding train
departs, wondering
if we should have got on it.

Old

I'm feeling old.
My body
feels the weight
of a swelling density
as I sit more loosely
in my sagging skin.

Mental gravity
fills me with a heaviness
that saps my strength,
drags my motivation
down.
My construction,
once robust, spirited,
strains under the burden
I've become.

I was nimble,
athletic,
now I stumble,
pathetic;
off-balance
just like my Dad,
believing I can still do it.

And yet
there is a deeper texture,
a kinder context
to my expansion;
perhaps some compassion
in the system
that shows me
aging gracefully
comes with new knowing.

Maybe a brightness peers
through the cracks
in my crumbling identity,
fractured by
my heightened curiosity
and a desire to evolve.
I feel a change of state,
my attitude expanding
as my heart speaks with resolve,
my body sighing
as I smile at the future
and the beckoning of
a peaceful wisdom.

I'm Scared of the Blender

I'm scared of the blender.

Maybe because it's black
and we call it Darth.

Or because it yells
thunderously
for exactly 35 seconds,
reveling in
the vivisection
of my blueberries
and yogurt,
as it creates
a contemptuous chaos
of angry purple.

Good job
it tastes great,
when I finally find
the courage
to take a sip,

a few feet away.

To Heal the Rift

We pour our perspective into
the space between us
like whitewater through a canyon,
mentally disputing everything
that resists,
or that doesn't fit our rigid position.

We shrink our ability to listen
as we wrap our parceled views so tightly
they are delivered with righteous finality
and blameless disdain,
offered from an imperfect prejudice
that confirms our bias.

We are blind to our beliefs
and ignorant of our attitudes.
Addicted to our warped perception
of the outlook of others
and all their distorted thinking,
we shout and shove and rail against
their misguided idiocy,
hooded and handcuffed by our
guiltless conscience.

How can we crack open
our own shutters?
Diminish our principles enough

to make room for others?
Cease the derision of different thinking?
How do we widen our narrow minds
and unseal our welded hearts?

How do we permit
a viewpoint from another angle?
How do we unfasten our certainty at being right
and break its hold on our padlocked mind?
Can we permit the light from others
to glimmer some hope
through a crack in our inflexible feelings?

The world we see is an interpretation
we testify is true.
Reluctant to stretch our understanding
or ease the firmness of our conclusions,
we refuse to refocus our outlook,
unwilling to admit any leakage
in the foundation of
our cemented ideals.

So, let us take a breath.

Let us soften the grip
on our reality.
Allow the gap between us
to become an opening,
a possibility
that permits us to change our challenge
from outward to inwards.

Helps us grow new buds
on the flower of our reasoning.
Adjust our position even slightly
so our new stance shifts the weight
of our posture.

Let us judge our own judgement
and see the limits of our thinking.
If we extend a hand,
we might expand our mind
and see another as different
rather than wrong,
as diverse rather than faulty.

Could we turn towards
rather than turning away?
Look for common ground
wherein grows
a combination of concepts?
Seek the beauty of the *and*
rather than the oppression of the *or*?

Let us heal the rift
by stealing our own hearts,
replacing conviction with compassion
and opinion with empathy.
We can hold a mirror to our flaws
and realize, perhaps for the first time,
that the tragic deficiency
lies not in others,
but in ourselves.

The Arc of Life

As my life
slowly flattens its arc
and my acute inclination
to intolerance
decreases,
the turmoil beneath
my calm exterior
settles to a simmer.

Verdicts withdraw—
so many conclusions
no longer required,
were never true.
So many habits
relax their knuckled grip.
My angry crowd
of beliefs
recede
on my ebbing tide,
uncovering
more of me
with each new moon.

I feel I am reflected
in an expanding mirror
of wet sand.
Refracting grains

of hard silica
roll over,
each one
a shining story,
a conviction,
a criticism,
an acquiescence.
A hope for
resolution
and the tranquility
of a still mind.

▌Wish

I wish I had the courage to ask you more often.

I wish you could hear my courage as much as my questions.

I wish I could share and let you in, unfold myself to
      your awareness.

I wish I could be clear with you, distinct from the noise and
      free of doubt.

I wish I could tell you how I feel beneath the layers of me.

I wish you could see the skins I wear and ask gently to
      unwrap them.

I wish you could see the world through my eyes, through
      my heart, with my intentions.

I wish I could see myself as you do, understand what you
      notice most.

And yet I know you accept me as I am, whole, without the
      hope, the expectation

of who you might want me to be.

I could wish for nothing more.

We Are Both

our scattered dreams and hopeless hope
our gifts and our wounds
the voices we try and the identities we assume
the veneers we wear and the truth underneath
the depths to which we sink and the heights to which we rise
our delusions and our aspirations
the kisses for our love and the silence for our sins
the fragments of our presence and the war for our attention
the loyalty of our tribe and the prejudice of our views
the triumph of our knowing and the corruption of
        our wisdom
the strength of our will and perseverance of our spirit
our cutting criticism and tender smiles
the shortcoming of our certainty and the blight of
our progress
the brittleness of our peace and the gore of our glory
the intolerance of our bias and the inaccuracy of
our assumptions
the love of our life and the hatred in our heart
the virtue of our intentions and the sadness of our failings
we are our darkness and our light
we are divergent and contrasting
and we become whole only when we integrate
and assimilate all our fragments
into a peaceful completeness

Holding Your Hand

It's not so much about
the perfect fit
of our snug hands,
the touch of your skin,
or the warmth
of the grip.
It's the feeling
that every crease,
every rivulet
of our palms
courses with meaning,
with gratitude
and anticipation,
as if our maps exactly
align,
our lifelines
intersecting,
marking the treasure
securely in the center.

The Skin of our Lives

We skim the surface,
skipping across the tense skin
of our industrious lives,
reluctant to reveal much
of what lies beneath.
We rarely share our depth,
preferring to protect ourselves
with a coating of pretense, as if
hiding a fear of being fully seen.

This self-preservation grows
from roots of deeply buried beliefs
that whisper,
I'm not good enough, or
I am flawed,
at the moments we need them least.

We have built versions of ourselves,
each with a mask to wear as we offer
only part of us to those who ask,
selecting which hat to wear, suitable
for the prevailing conditions.

Such habits we have formed
for so long, these accidental deceits
parade reliably, with a brightness of costume
designed to conceal our inner world,

ensuring others see only the imitation
we present, while we avoid
or hold close our real feelings.

We conceal, knowingly or not,
the sadness of our shame,
the meanness of our misery,
the agony of our anger,
or even the desire to be loved recklessly,
willing it to crash like a train
through the self-creation
of our tiring lives.

Why do we disguise the truth of us?
Is it because we're afraid
to face it ourselves,
or expose it to others?
We often have a vague notion,
an uneasy feeling,
something's not right,
that we are not whole,
not everything we could be,
but we readily ignore this
unwanted distraction
from our trudging tenure.

What if we lifted the lid?
What if we looked?
What if we faced the mirror,
submitted to our reflection
and stepped purposefully through it

to experience ourselves,
exposed and vulnerable?

What if we leaned in
and learned
to love ourselves, just as we are,
to believe in ourselves fully,
with compassion and kindness?

Surely this act of self-tenderness
would nurture our souls,
free us from the chains
of our minds, and let us shine
our brilliance into the world
for all to see,
for everyone to feel,
and for us to recognize
as the meaning of life.

Waking

In the uncertain light
of morning,
a clearing
subconscious fog
quietly uncovers
my dim attention,
dissolves my disorientation
as a dream evaporates
into a sense of something.

My waking notions
arise unhurriedly
from deep sleep
into consciousness,
to discover themselves
and divulge
to my noticing.

My awareness,
barely warm,
places a soft hand
on my forehead.
Fleeting thoughts
and questions
dance

as I drift
to a state
with hints of promise,

only to begin
a groggy debate
with the embrace
of snug darkness.

Part 3:

NATURE

A Poet's Wish

Let my feet
be firmly planted,
toes digging
into the warm soil,
thirsty as roots.

Let my trunk be strong,
arteries and capillaries
gorged with
the sap of life.
Let my arms
spread as branches,
my hands reaching out,
fingers stretching
as supple stems
seeking . . .

Let each letter
form new buds
that sprout into leaves,
each a beautifully curved
consonant,
a veined vowel,
trembling in anticipation
of a fluency
of foliage.

Let my natural alchemy
transform sunlight
into radiance,
a nurturing
of fresh language.
An expression of life,
a fervent articulation of hope
through prose full of growth.

Let this canopy
delight you,
holding you safe
as you lean into its
permanence.
Climb into the limbs
and see the world from there,
wide-eyed
at the wonder
of it all.

World Wind

if I pause for just a moment
I can feel the earth breathing
I can hear life
rustling through the birch
and aspen
in a flow of whispers
each leaf's vibration
a quivering note
giving the wind
a voice
as if the branches bow
in reverence
to the exhalation
forming chords
that blend into
a composition of song
stirring through the grove
chilling my face
reminding me
to gently place my awareness
on my own breath
to tune in
to my aliveness
inhaling the music
the same air

the world breathes
drawing in the beauty
of the moment
and smiling quietly
at the graceful connection
of it all

Where the Forest Meets the Sea

A boneyard of wood,
strewn as awkward carcasses,
stabs the shoulder of the shore
while uncountable pebbles
shrug their roundness
against the pale timbers,
echoing past furies,
all cemented
with a transient sand
of coarsely crushed shells.

Sunburned brown-black rocks
grip the coast
with calloused knuckles,
their backs slapped
with unrelenting surf
and a conclusion of foamy spray.

The blue-grey churn
dips and stands,
pitches wilfully against the
clutching stone,
sacrificed in pointless rage
as if reaching
for the stranded lumber

scattered at the feet
of the startled spruce
and the reddened fingers
of arbutus.

Close by,
the conifers stand and sway,
a deep green
of exclamation marks,
sentinels against the beauty
of the wrath below,
guarding their dead
as they patiently wait
to join them.

After Autumn

It was an irritable day.
Petulant, it threw a tantrum
at the ignorant world.
A paper-edge wind blew
along talcum sidewalks,
dry as broken glass,
scuffing the clean, arid powder
into crystal snow dunes.

The bitter breeze sandblasted
the town,
frenzied the exhausts of
crunching, plastic-hard cars
as they groaned and snaked,
cold-blooded, along the sharp streets.

Bleak, biting gusts
swatted the huddled,
preoccupied folk,
their watering eyes averted,
innocent victims of the season.

Reluctant cirrus,
high and thin,
whispered white
against the steel sky
as they raced away,
bringing winter clawing behind
with frigid intent.

Glacier

Crawling
from corrie'd womb,
this savage sculptor,
patient parasite,
tears its craggy bed
with terrible sloth.

Sneering a
crevassed smile
of chapped lips
and crooked teeth,
it slowly carves
down the grey mountain.

Arching vertebrae
crack with cold
as saliva dribbles
from its frigid snout.

Deathly pale,
it heaves and sighs,
swallowing its course
with crumbling hunger
until satiated.

Then, when warmth returns,
it quietly melts
into its own cold scars,
dripping through
the debris of its sculpture
in despairing finality.

Oregon Shore

Coastal hills
swathed in yellow gorse
paint a fresh picture
beyond each wave-sculpted headland.

Tufts of swordfern and thimbleberry
carpet the feet
of hunched spruce
draping seaward
towards the rocky conclusions,
which squat in resignation,
gnawed and nibbled
by the unrelenting swell.

Blackened basalt bastions
encrusted with barnacles
like crunchy frosting
defy the hungry surf,
their backs green and dark,
their faces windblown
and pitted like old sailors.

Sneaky beaches
hide in crabby coves
littered with whalebone driftwood.
From sienna sandstone bluffs
tears of agate spill

onto the endless silica dunes
snaking across
the rolled-out pastry sand.

Hidden lagoons lie soft,
rippling with agreeable wrinkles;
bullfrogs grunt their acquiescence
into the apricot evening
while the grand old lady
with foaming petticoats
strokes the shore
and goes forever on.

Children of the Clouds

The stolid cows lie down
and turn their patient, pooled eyes
to the sky.
Leaves curl expectantly
and flutter in the signalling wind.
Small things scurry as they smell the change.

In the distance, she approaches,
her leaden curtain drawing closer.
Ashen pillars support her pillowy weight.
Fluffy washerwoman, this mother cloud
spreads sheets of grey upon the green beneath.
Heavy and ponderous, she reaches down,
stroking the ground with a sodden hand.
Within her damp bosom
droplet seeds pause,
waiting wetly to be sown
until they release
and take the plunge.

The shrouded cloud advances
sprinkling the first petulant plops.
Droplets dash the ground
as people dash for cover.
Soon the dripping woman
releases her children like an uncaring parent;
this billowing matron with a sorrowful expression

frowns her tears onto the dampening earth
as if weeping at her loss.

Her sadness holds the dark world captive,
but her drizzled eyes heed not
the soggy, vulnerable landscape.
Sullen stone dwellings hunch down
with reflective slate roofs
as if considering their future.
The still, silk-back mare
blows plumes of mist into the wet air.

Soggy sheep,
cautious cats.
Silver straight roads lie rigid
like metal canals.
All is splashy cascading chaos.

These cloud children
pour liquid life into the greedy earth,
which drinks and dribbles, spilling
capillaries of water, chattering and babbling,
blood of the soil,
towards bloated river veins
which carry their precious charges to the sea.

Respite, and the sky cracks open
like an unshuttered window.
A timid haze glows tentatively
behind the retreating, silver brood.
The dripping stops,

the trickling starts,
and the squinting sun looks down
upon the streaky, slippery wake.

The earth quietly steams like a Sunday roast,
satiated, as the golden alchemist
begins to turn droplets into diamonds.
Sparkling flowers lift their heads
and the battered spider
surveys with wonder his jewelled web,
hung with a thousand mirrors.

A phoenix of creatures arises from the dregs
and ventures through the slick, cut-glass grass.
An insect drinks from a magnifying glob
then spreads its wings to dry.

Ocean - Ebb

Her deep wisdom
lies beneath
our knowing,
despite her treasured state.

We only skim the surface
with nervous pleasure
as we seek to understand
this tidal mother-essence.
The watery frontier
we willfully abuse,
poisoning with plastic
as we selfishly steal from
her dwindling stocks.

There is no helm for men,
despite our worthy vessels
and arrogance of craft.
Our reluctance to remain
in her embrace
bred from respect
for the give and take
of the waves
and currents,
knowing we are
mere hostages
to the pitiless swell.

Life source
and stealer
just the same,
a dealer in the incessant
ebb and flow of living.
She presents a haven
for ocean creatures
and a burial ground
of limestone layers
down in the cold
of death.

Circumspect
to the persistent disturbance,
she always attempts
to return to her level self,
a healing ritual
as reliable as gravity.

Even the crashing amplitude
of waves and troughs
in endless regurgitation
is anchored by
her irrefutable flatness.
As if the frothing
and splashing
would distract us
from her deep
and silent calm.
Eased by a sinking moon,
she settles resolute,

the unwavering source
to which all water returns,
her mercurial expressions
eternally in motion
even when tranquil.

While at the far edges
of her ebbing emotions,
temporary echoes of skin
lie in apprehensive frowns
of beached sand,
so beautifully sculpted
by the indecision
of the rippling waves
as she patiently inhales
the next tide.

Ocean - Flow

Across the vast texture
of relentless motion,
her seas liquidly mirror
a grey-blue sky,
or sparkle specks of sunlight
while braiding together
endless saline seifs,
cupping momentary sails
along the arching crests.

This constant flux
of instantaneous miracles
pours perpetually
over itself,
reshaping
to stretch the swells
into foam-crusted patterns
of molten bark.

A waterscape
only temporarily mapped
as the warming of latitudes
and the insistent trade winds
transfer their power
to dishevel the broad surface
of the deep blackness.

Ceaselessly transforming
her tidal beauty,
she demands no admiration
for her curves,
yet in an instant
shows every emotion
from a ruffled calm
of sliding shadows
to the stretched white intake
of white crests
crashing down
in detonating rage.
A buoyant hope,
or mercurial irritation,
so many moods
we cannot begin to fathom
from the wrinkles and creases
of such an ancient face.

This loyal mother
expresses only pure response
to what is conveyed.
Faithful servant
to the turns of the world,
she writhes in torment,
pushing the deathly trembles
of the Earth
with immense purpose
and ruthless compliance.

Waiting in the Rain

Pearls of water
shower
from the streetlamp
like suspended necklaces.

I wait wet-caged
on the corner.
Will she come?

Yellow light
pools
in the hopeless drizzle.
My mind swims.
Should I shuffle
to one more pool
and back?

My socks are wet.
Tickets and gift
dampen in my pocket.

One more pool?

The
minutes
drip
slowly
from
my
wrist.

May Morning, England 1976

A stumbling, sleep-eyed figure
gropes downstairs,
dreaming his way into
a creaky, waking kitchen.
Lino clutches his warm, bare feet
like cold, hard mud.
The window blind protests
as its squinting eyes are opened
to the inquisitive dawn.

In the damp garden,
the cherry tree scatters
pink blossom snowfall
onto the dark earth-solemn soil.
A clean, sweet, cut grass smell
unfolds in the quiet breeze,
punctuated by pigeon coos
and the friendly clank of milk bottles.

Storm clouds gather in the
dark, Bill's-mother distance.
Echoing the car-growl,
kid-shout of the village,
a short-wave blast of unreality

screams music into the soft air
until the sound is dimmed,
and the morning news reveals
fresh tragedies.

Hot and friendly,
the first gulp
percolates life
through a somnolent system,
raising energy enough
to collect the morning paper
and the milk
from the doorstep.

The Lark's Song

Half-waking, when the dawn is near,
Through morning mists a song I hear.
And while the air's yet still and cold,
A wondrous music doth unfold.

The lark, uprising with the sun,
Heralds with song the day begun,
And winged music fills the air
With love, and with a beauty rare.

And who ordained each happy note
That trembles from the tiny throat ?
And where's the heart that deaf could be
To such exquisite harmony ?

From what divine height of sweet sound
Was such transcending music found ?
Each bell-like note comes from above
To share with all its song of love.

For God decreed that melody
Should ever in thy spirit be,
And so, sweet lark, give forth full tongue
That all might hear thy beauteous song.

Dorothy Helen Banton
31st May, 1951
Age 20

The Author

Christopher Jones emigrated to Canada from England in 1981, seeking adventure and opportunity at the age of 23. He brought with him a few poems he had written as a teenager, born from a love of language and a poet's heart. It took nearly 40 years before his poetic artistry found the time and space to fully reveal itself, for his poems to escape and be captured at the same time. *The Nature of Humans* is Chris's first collection of poetry, written while growing a leadership development company with his business partner and loving wife, Lisa Scott. Chris has always tried to evolve himself throughout his life, which has fueled his passion for supporting the personal growth and professional development of others. Personal growth is the predominant theme of the book. Chris lives in Calgary, Alberta, within sight of the glorious Rocky Mountains. He has two loving and supportive adult children, Thom and Charlotte.

CPSIA information can be obtained
at www.ICGtesting.com
Printed in the USA
BVHW070204231021
619493BV00001B/31

9 781039 116702